DIVE I...

Splash

KINGDOM

A LIFE SAVING MUSICAL FOR KIDS

BY PAM ANDREWS
ARRANGED BY BARNY ROBERTSON

Lillenas PUBLISHING COMPANY

Box 419572, Kansas City, MO 64141

www.lillenas.com

CONTENTS

Overture

Splash Kingdom
Dive
Come on in, the Water's Fine

Arranged by Barny Robertson

PLEASE NOTE: Copying of this product is NOT covered by CCLI licenses. For CCLI information call 1-800-234-2446.

6

8

9

Splash Kingdom

John 7:38

Words and Music by
PAM ANDREWS, GARY SIMMONS
and ROGER GREER
Arranged by Barny Robertson

KID 1: Come on, everyone! It's time to dive in to Splash Kingdom.

KID 2: Right! Grab your goggles and your suntan lotion and join us at the best water park in the land. *(The choir enters from all parts of the auditorium.)*

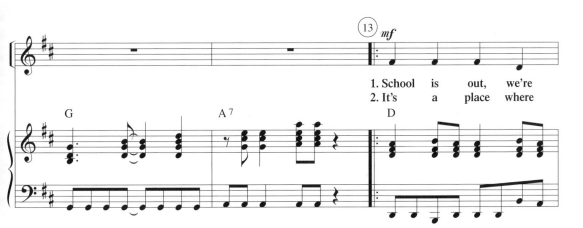

14

no-where else at all   you'll find

hang   out,   hang   out

A♭   A♭/B♭   E♭   E♭/G   E♭/B♭

More fun than   slid - ing down the side   of   a

at   the mall,_____   Slid -   ing,

E♭   Fm7   E♭/G   (58) A♭

gi - ant wa - ter slide;   We can hard - ly wait un - til we

slid -   ing,   ah,

A♭   F7

Scene 1

(At the end of the song the cast meets at center stage. Peter is on the lifeguard stand and the lifeguard team is standing next to him.)

SANDY: Like, I am so excited! Here we are, Sandy Shore and Shelly Bubbles, and all of our friends totally here at Splash Kingdom! Awesome!

DEW: *(carrying a surfboard)* Hey! Let's go catch a wave and ride that curl.

KIDS: Yeah!!!!

DEW: Dude! I've died and gone to heaven!

SHELLY: *(southern accent)* Why, if it isn't Dew Drop, the best surfer anywhere.

DEW: Dew Drop's the name and surfin's my game!

SHELLY: I don't know about y'all, but I've been waitin' for this day all year! We almost had to go to that other water park. You know, the one that's so terribly hot! *(fans herself)*

(Tanner appears wearing flippers, goggles, swimmies, and a floating toy around his waist.)

TANNER: Hi, everyone! Sorry I'm a little late. I had to make a quick stop by the bank to get some spending money for the park. The first ride's on me…Tanner C. Fish. *(shows money to kids)*

KIDS: Yea!!!!

TANNER: Ahhh, Splash Kingdom. Truly a wonderful sight even to a Blueblood. I, Tanner C. Fish am ready to rumble.

SANDY: Like, you look more like you are ready to stumble. Tanner, what's deal with all the swim attire? You look like a walking toy display.

TANNER: I made a quick run through the Tall Mart Department Store and picked up a few items to assist me in my day at Splash Kingdom. For the Fish family, first class is the only way.

SANDY: Really! Like, could it be that you're just afraid of the water?

SHELLY: Well, he did have that incident last year.

DEW: Ouch! Dude. No more diving for pennies in a wading pool.

SHELLY: *(looks at the gate)* Look everyone! It's past 10:00 o'clock and the gate is still closed.

DEW: *(shakes the gate)* Hey! Open up! Let us in!

SANDY: Yeah, like, let us in!

KIDS: Open up!!! Let us in!

TANNER: Wait! Wait! I, Tanner C. Fish, will use my influence with the management to rectify this situation. Hello? Hello? *(shakes the fence and yells)* Let us in!!

SHELLY: *(disgusted)* Some influence. Look, there's a lifeguard. Maybe he can help. *(to Peter)* Excuse us, sir,

PETER: Can I help you?

SHELLY: We're all here ready to have a day of fun at Splash Kingdom.

PETER: Great, we'll be glad to have you. I'm Peter, the supervising lifeguard in charge of the front gate and this is my assistant, Gabriel, and our fine Splash Kingdom team of lifeguards. We run the "Daywatch" shift here at Splash Kingdom. *(climbs off the lifeguard stand)*

SANDY: Whatever! So what's with the gate. Shouldn't you be open by now?

KIDS: Yeah!!!

PETER: Do you have a reservation?

SANDY: Who ever heard of needing a reservation to like enter a water park? Duh!

DEW: Radical, my mom keeps saying she has reservations about me! Does that count, Pete?

PETER: No, this reservation had to be made personally with our Chief Executive Officer, Jesus Christ.

TANNER: I am Tanner C. Fish of the Boston Fish Family and I always have a standing reservation.

PETER: No one has a standing reservation at Splash Kingdom. There is only one way to enter. Your name must be found in our reservation book. We call this our Book of Life. *(points to the Book of Life)*

TANNER: Now, we're getting somewhere. I'm sure you'll find my name. Tanner C. Fish is on all the finest registries. *(to kids)* Don't worry, everyone, my name talks. I'll have us inside this gate in no time.

GABRIEL: *(looks in the book)* Tanner C. Fish...No, sorry, sir. I don't see Tanner C. Fish listed.

TANNER: There must be some mistake. How rude!

SANDY: *(pushes Tanner aside)* Like, I'm Sandy Shore. Gabe, could you like surf through the pages for my name?

GABRIEL: *(looks in the book)* No, I'm sorry.

SANDY: Like, bummer!

SHELLY: How about me? I'm Shelly Bubbles. Do you see my little ole' name?

GABRIEL: *(looks in the book)* Uh let's see. Betty Bubbles...Candy Bubbles...Sharie Bubbles... Tiny Bubbles. Sorry, no Shelly Bubbles.

SHELLY: How distressing!

DEW: Gabe, Dude, do you eyeball the name Dew Drop?

GABRIEL: *(looks in the book)* Yes, I see some Drops. There is a Daisy Drop and a Dudley Drop.

DEW: Cool, dude! They're my grandparents.

GABRIEL: But, again, I'm sorry to say, I see no Dew Drop.

PETER: We are sorry. You simply can't get in without a reservation.

TANNER: This is unbelievable! Who is this CEO...Jesus Christ? My dad works with every top executive in the country. He must know my dad.

PETER: My boss knows everyone...but do you know Him? That is the question.

SANDY: Hey, like, couldn't you look one more time?

PETER: I'll be glad to check again, but if your name is not in the Book of Life you may not enter. Sorry! No exceptions!

Do You Know Him?

Words and Music by
PAM ANDREWS
Arranged by Barny Robertson

Solemn ♩ = ca. 78

CD: 8

Solo (Peter)
mp ③

I'll take an-oth-er look in-side our Gold-en Book of Life, I'll glad-ly check a-gain to make quite sure that I am right.

(spoken) ⑦

No, I'm a-fraid your name is ab-sent,

CD: 9

Faster ♩ = ca. 106

no - where to be seen. To en - ter you must know our Mas - ter,

Je - sus Christ the King! PETER: Maybe our lifeguard team can help.

Choir

Do you

know, know, know the Man? (Do you know, know, know the Man?) Do you

*OPTION: Divide choir into two groups, one group sings the echos (part in parenthesis)

CD: 10

Choir

___ Him?   Do you

Dm

28

know, know, know the Man?   (Do you know, know, know the Man?)   Do you

Dm

CD: 11 1st time

know, know, know the Man?   (Do you know, know, know the Man?)

Dm

32 *Optional solo*

2. Do you know the Man___ who raised up Laz' - rus from the dead?   Five
3. Do you know the Man___ who on the cross for us did die   To

Dm

CD: 15

(Yeah!)_____ Do you know, know, know the Man?

Em

(Do_____ you know__ Him?) 4. Do you know the Man who on the

Em

third day left the tomb? He won the vic - t'ry o - ver death and

Em   Am

He's re - turn - ing soon! Do you know__ Him? Know, know, know, know, know.

B7   Em

Scene 2

SHELLY: Thank you for sharing such a great history lesson with us all.

SANDY: But, like, we don't have all day.

TANNER: Let me try another angle. *(pulls out his platinum bank card)* I'm sure my platinum card might help. *(waves his credit card in front of Peter's nose)* Come on, name your price. Money's no object. The sky's the limit when you are dealing with a Fish.

PETER: That's the funny thing about Splash Kingdom. The admission is free. Someone else paid for your admission many years ago.

TANNER: Come on, money talks. *(pushes card in Peter's hand)*

PETER: *(holds up his hand)* Money is silent at the gates of Splash Kingdom. To enter, you must be certified by passing Lifesaving 101. That and only that will introduce you to my boss and open the gate. You see, He is the gate. You can only enter through Him.

DEW: OK, if passing this Lifesaving 101 gig will get us in, let's give it a ride.

ALL: Sure thing! Great!

PETER: Lifesaving 101 has three basic steps to certification. "A," admit you have sinned; "B," believe God loves you and sent His Son and our CEO, Jesus, to save you from your sin; and "C," claim Jesus as your own personal lifeguard and Savior. You might call this class the "ABC's to Salvation."

DEW: Hey, Pete, why do we really need a lifeguard? *(points to himself)* This dude is a great swimmer. I swim like a fish…*(to Tanner)* no pun intended.

TANNER: *(defensive)* I, Tanner C. Fish am also an excellent swimmer.

DEW: Your only problem is that you *(holds his nose as he speaks the remainder of the line)* have to hold your nose when you swim.

PETER: Lifesaving 101 teaches you to swim in living water. Lifeguard Team, come show us the plan.

Lifesaving 101

John 10:9; Acts 16:31

Words and Music by
PAM ANDREWS, GARY SIMMONS
and ROGER GREER
Arranged by Barny Robertson

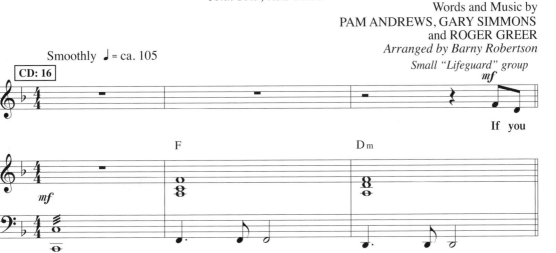

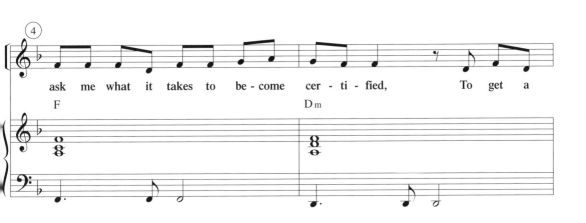

34

36

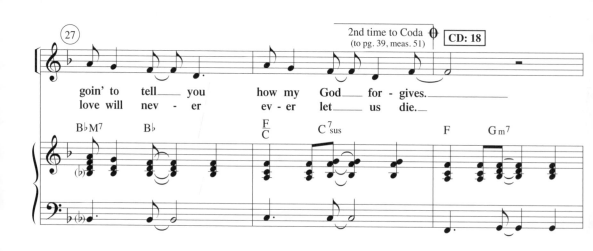

life will change____ for good,_____ And you'll

learn to live____ each day the way____ you should.___

CD: 21

Choir *f*

Life - sav - ing

mf

Ba ba ba ba

44

Scene 3

PETER: My boss has provided a great textbook to guide you as you learn. *(holds up a Bible)*

TANNER: I read the Times and Wall Street Journal, but I don't believe I've ever seen this book.

PETER: This is the Bible.

SANDY: *(the kids open the Bible)* Like! Look at all those tiny words!

SHELLY: This is almost as long as "Gone with the Wind."

DEW: Dude! My grandparents were always reading the Bible. Granny knew a scripture for everything. In fact, every time this surfer dude *(points to himself)* got out of line, she had me copying those Ten Commandments.

TANNER: *(holds up Bible)* OK, we've got our textbook. Let's get started. *(points to watch)* Time is ticking away.

PETER: You're right about that. Many a person has missed Splash Kingdom simply because they kept putting off their certification. Let's begin. "A", admit that you have sinned. Gabriel, could you read Romans 3:23 from our textbook?

GABRIEL: Yes, sir. *(reads the scripture from his New Testament)* "For all have sinned and fall short of the glory of God."

SANDY: Sin? Like what is sin?

PETER: Sin is something that you do which is against Jesus.

TANNER: I doubt I've ever sinned. I attended the Junior Cotillion, you know.

PETER: Everyone sins. Everyone needs to be forgiven. Think about it! Did you ever glance over at someone's test at school? Or did you ever take something that wasn't yours? At that moment you were guilty of sin.

I'm Guilty

A Sinner's Prayer

Romans 3:23

Words and Music by
PAM ANDREWS, GARY SIMMONS
and ROGER GREER
Arranged by Barny Robertson

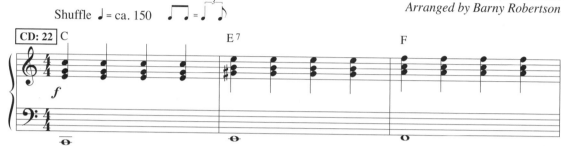

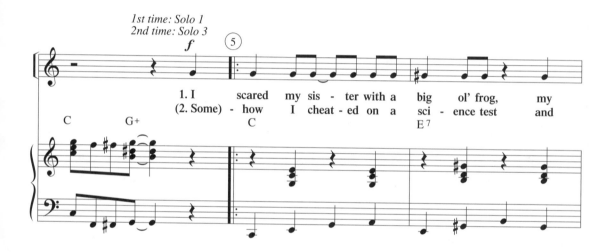

how we got in the mess we're in, I'm guilt-y,
is no one in a "no sin" zone, I'm guilt-y,

I am guilt - y,

F   C   D

(to pg. 46, meas. 5)

CD: 24 1st time
CD: 26 2nd time

Solo 3

guilt-y of do - ing wrong.
guilt-y of do - ing wrong.

do - ing wrong.

2. Some -

G   G⁶   C   G+

E - ven though we're

C   C♯   D   D♯   E⁷

50

bound to sin I have good news to-day;_____ Christ

E7   A7

Je - sus died to wash our sins a - way._____

D7   D13   G

Trust Him as your Sav - ior and___ re -

G   G♭ F   E7

ceive His sav - ing grace._____ He'll wipe that guilt - y

A7   D7

we're   guilt-y,   I'm

we   are   guilt - y,

guilt-y,   guilt-y of do - ing wrong.____

I   am   guilt - y,   do - ing wrong.____

Scene 4

SHELLY: Goodness, I'm afraid I sin all the time. There's no hope in my ever getting into Splash Kingdom.

SANDY: Ditto. Like, I try to do things right, but things just go wrong. Bummer.

DEW: Hey! I'm the guilty one. It's tough keepin' this surfer dude's head straight!

TANNER: When you put it that way, I guess even a Fish makes mistakes from time to time.

PETER: Great! You have all passed the first step. You have admitted to your sin. Now, you are ready for the second step. You must, "B," believe God loves you and sent His Son, Jesus to save you from your sin. Just look at Tanner…he has all that gear on to make him feel safe.

TANNER: *(indignant)* I'm not afraid. A Fish is simply always prepared.

DEW: Come on, Tanner! Cough it up! What's with the water wings?

TANNER: Ok, ok, I guess I'm really wearing all this lifesaving gear 'cause I'm afraid something bad might happen to me.

PETER: Everyone has things they're afraid of, but, the great thing about fear is that Jesus came to take our fears…if we just believe in Him. Gabriel, find John 3:16 in our textbook and read it to us.

GABRIEL: *(over music)* "For God so loved the world that He gave His one and only Son, that whoever believes in Him shall not perish but have eternal life."

We Believe in Jesus Christ

John 3:16

Words and Music by
PAM ANDREWS
Arranged by Barny Robertson

56

58

build - ing us a man - sion on those shin - y streets of gold!

G⁷sus   G⁷   Gm¹¹   C⁷

40

We be - lieve, we be - lieve, we be -

Am¹¹   E♭⁷ D⁷sus   G   Am⁷

lieve in Je - sus Christ. We be - lieve, we be - lieve that He

G/B   C   G/B   Em

44

paid for us the price. We be - lieve, we be - lieve, we be -

A⁹   A⁷   D⁷sus   G   Am⁷

Scene 5

DEW: I don't know about you guys, but I'm feeling pretty good!

SHELLY: I'm filling with "happy thoughts". My heart is bubbling with joy!

SANDY: Massive! Learning is so, like, cool. What's left, Peter?

PETER: Lesson three in Lifesaving 101 says you must, "C," claim Jesus as your Savior. Gabriel, find Romans 10:13 in our textbook and read it for me.

DEW: Radical, Gabe. Let your fingers do the walkin for ya.

(kids laugh)

GABRIEL: Here it is. Romans 10:13 says, "Everyone who calls on the name of the Lord will be saved."

DEW: Do you mean to tell me that all I have to do is ask and this Jesus Dude will come?

PETER: Yes, Dew, and He will open the gate. He wants everyone to enter Splash Kingdom. The rich, the poor, the weak, the strong. Jesus is the living water that saves us.

TANNER: Am I, Tanner C. Fish, welcome to swim in this water?

PETER: Sure, thing, Tanner. Just ask and you will receive.

Living Water

Romans 10:13

Words and Music by
PAM ANDREWS
Arranged by Barny Robertson

62

(to pg. 61, meas. 7)

Wa - ter come down,_____ Je - sus the Liv - ing

Am   G/B   C   D/C

Wa - ter come down,_____ Je - sus the Liv - ing

Am   G/B   C   D/C

Wa - ter come down_____ on me.

Am   G/B   G2

G2

Scene 6

PETER: Congratulations! You have all passed Lifesaving 101 and are now certified.

ALL: Yea! Right! Cool!

SHELLY: Gabriel, how about checking to see if our names are in the Book of Life?

GABRIEL: Sure thing. Let's see…Shelly Bubbles. There it is! *(turns the page)* Sandy Shore… yes, it's also here.

SHELLY AND SANDY: Yes! Yes! Yes! *(scream happily, hugging and jumping up and down)*

DEW: Hey! How about checking for my name, Gabe?

GABRIEL: Yes! I see it right there between Daisy Drop and Dudley Drop.

DEW: Cool, Pete! I can't wait to tell my Granny.

TANNER: Hey, wait. What about me? I don't suppose you see a Tanner C. Fish on that list?

GABRIEL: Sure do, Tanner.

TANNER: Look at me. I'm not afraid anymore! I think I might even lose these water wings. *(takes off his swim toys)*

SANDY: Like, cool, Tanner. You looked like a bubble in all that stuff.

GABRIEL: Our Textbook says in Proverbs 18:4, "The words of a man's mouth are deep waters, but the fountain of wisdom is a bubbling brook."

SHELLY: That's just how I feel inside. I'm bubblin' with joy!

Bubbling Joy

Proverbs 18:4

Words and Music by
PAM ANDREWS
Arranged by Barny Robertson

70

74

joy,   bub - bl-ing,   bub-bl-ing joy._____   Joy,   bub - bl-ing joy,__

bub - bl-ing   Je-sus in my heart brings   bub-bl-ing joy!_____

CD: 44

76

Scene 7

PETER: You have been certified and are now ready to enter Splash Kingdom. Gabriel, open the gate.

(Gabriel and the other lifeguards open the gate.)

SANDY: Like, I don't know what to ride first!

SHELLY: I think I might surf down Eternal Life Mountain.

SANDY: Gee, that sounds cool! I might ride the Rapture Raft Ride.

DEW: I'm heading straight to Forever Falls.

TANNER: I know where I'm going. I'm going to take a trip down that River of Life. Come on! Let's go!

Dive

Revelation 22:1-2

Words and Music by
STEVEN CURTIS CHAPMAN
Arranged by Barny Robertson

But we will nev-er know the awe - some pow - er of the grace of God

Un - til we let our-selves get swept a - way in - to this ho - ly flood.

84

Scene 8

(At this point in the script, you could have an invitation using the song "I Have Decided To Follow Jesus," if you so desire.)

PETER: Come join us at Splash Kingdom. The certification is easy. "A," admit you have sinned; "B," believe God loves you and sent His Son Jesus to save you from your sins; and "C," claim Jesus as your Savior. Then, share the good news of Jesus with everyone. Come on! Join us in Splash Kingdom!

Finale

Come on in, the Water's Fine
Splash Kingdom
We Believe in Jesus Christ
Dive

Matthew 28:19-20

Arranged by Barny Robertson

"Splash Kingdom"

see___ the sign, Splash King-dom, Splash King-dom,

see___ the sign, Splash King-dom, Splash King-dom,

Load 'em up, we're leav-in' to-day. Splash

Splash

King-dom, Splash King-dom,

King-dom, Splash King-dom,

94

96 CD: 58

Curtain Call

Splash Kingdom
Dive

Arranged by Barny Robertson

100

CD: 60

I'm div - in' in,   I'm go - in' deep,   in   o - ver my head. I wan - na be

CD: 61 Wave Sounds SFX for use between songs. You may want to copy it 3 or 4 times to use for a prolonged sound.

PRODUCTION NOTES

Setting

The set of Splash Kingdom is the front gate of a water park. You will want to use the pattern found in the Splash Kingdom Director's Resource Kit to create the water park backdrop. The set also has a red lifeguard stand, a movable gate, and a book stand for "The Book of Life." For more details about the set please consult the Splash Kingdom Video or the Splash Kingdom Director's Resource Kit.

Casting Ideas

This musical is perfect for both the large and small choir. You may do the musical as written utilizing only the main characters if you have a smaller choir. If your choir is large, you may want to include the optional casting ideas with the main characters. Divide parts, add solos, be creative. Give everyone a part if possible. You will have better attendance and greater interest from the children and parents if each child has a special part. Please the Lord and the kids!

Cast

Peter the Lifeguard

Tanner C. Fish—rich kid

Sandy Shore—cheerleader

Kid 1

Shelly Bubbles—Southern girl

Dew Drop—beach kid

Gabriel

Kid 2

Optional Cast

The following are all non-speaking, acting roles.

Mary - Do You Know Him? vs. 1

Joseph - Do You Know Him? vs. 1

Lazarus - Do You Know Him? vs. 2

Small boy - Do You Know Him? vs. 2

Soldier - Do You Know Him? vs. 3

Woman at the tomb - Do You Know Him? vs. 4

3 ABC Card kids - Lifesaving 101

Brother - I'm Guilty vs. 1

Sister - I'm Guilty vs. 1
Girl who cheats - I'm Guilty vs. 2
Friend of girl who cheats - I'm Guilty 2
Boy or girl who says bad word - I'm Guilty vs. 2
Boy or girl who reacts to bad word -I'm Guilty vs. 2

Specialty Movement Artists

Note: The movement for the Specialty Aritsts is found in the Splash Kingdom
Resource Kit or on the Splash Kingdom Video
    Splash Kingdom Beach Kids
    Lifesaving 101 Muscle Men Surfers
    Living Water Movement Artists
    Bubblin's Song Surprise Partners

Costumes

Peter the Lifeguard	Lifeguard t-shirt, soccer shorts, tennis shoes or beach shoes, whistle, clipboard
Shelly Bubbles	Splash Kingdom t-shirt, soccer shorts, tennis shoes or beach shoes, feather boa, feather fan
Tanner C. Fish	Splash Kingdom t-shirt, soccer shorts, tennis shoes or beach shoes, pouch for money and credit card, silly swim ring around waist, goggles, fins, swimmies
Dew Drop	Splash Kingdom t-shirt, soccer shorts, tennis shoes or beach shoes, wild spiked hair, could be a wig, surf board
Sandy Shore	Splash Kingdom t-shirt, soccer shorts, tennis shoes or beach shoes, cheerleader pom poms, bright bow in her hair
Gabriel	Lifeguard t-shirt, soccer shorts, tennis shoes or beach shoes
Kid 1 & 2	Splash Kingdom t-shirt, soccer shorts, tennis shoes or beach shoes

Optional Cast Costumes

Mary - blue biblical costume
Joseph - beige biblical costume
Lazarus - white biblical costume—should look like a mummy
Small boy - child biblical costume
Soldier - biblical soldier costume
Women at the tomb - biblical costume
3 ABC Card kids - Lifeguard t-shirt, soccer shorts, tennis shoes or beach shoes
Brother - Splash Kingdom t-shirt, soccer shorts, tennis shoes or beach shoes
Sister - Splash Kingdom t-shirt, soccer shorts, tennis shoes or beach shoes
Girl who cheats - Splash Kingdom t-shirt, soccer shorts, tennis shoes or beach shoes
Friend of person who cheats - Splash Kingdom t-shirt, soccer shorts, tennis shoes or beach shoes
Boy or girl who says bad word - Splash Kingdom t-shirt, soccer shorts, tennis shoes or beach shoes
Boy or girl who reacts to bad word - Splash Kingdom t-shirt, soccer shorts, tennis shoes or beach shoes

Specialty Movement Artists

Splash Kingdom Beach Kids - Splash Kingdom t-shirt, soccer shorts, tennis shoes or beach shoes
Lifesaving 101 Muscle Men Surfers - Splash Kingdom t-shirt, soccer shorts, muscle man sleeves, surf boards
Living Water Movement Artists - long, blue and silver metallic fringe on the sleeves of blue jackets
Bubblin's Song Surprise Partners - fake legs and feet are placed around the waist of one child. One child sits on the waist of the other. The children flip up and down during the song revealing the pretend legs and feet.

The Set Design

In front of the Splash Kingdom backdrop starting at stage right should be the choir risers. To the left fo the risers should be the lifeguard stand. Left of the stand at center stage should be the gate; left of the gate should be the Book of Life and to the left of the book there are additional choir risers. In front of these props, should be the actors, the main characters and soloists microphones. See placement on next page.

Splash Kingdom backdrop

risers   lifeguard stand   gate   Book of Life   risers

        actors   main characters   soloists
                                                                      X X X

Props

Swimming props - rings, beach towels, beach balls, noodles, surf boards
The Book of Life
Bible
Lifesaving rings - 1 per child—to spin during Lifesaving 101
Water shakers - 2 per child—to be used during Living Water
Play money
Fake credit card
Sunglasses
Bubbles

Optional Props

Baby Jesus doll
Cot for Lazarus
Basket of loaves and fishes
Life-size cross
Round tomb stone - large round piece of Styrofoam spray painted gray
Lifesaving 101 cards
        A. Admit you have sinned.
        B. Believe God loves you.
        C. Claim Jesus as your Savior.
Stuffed frog
Stuffed dog
2 clipboards for science tests
2 pencils

Solos

Do You Know Him?

    Solo 1—Peter   Solo 2—Lifeguard 1
    Solo 3—Lifeguard 2   Solo 4—Lifeguard 3
Lifesaving 101
    Intro Solo—Lifeguard Trio   Solo 1—Lifeguard 4
    Solo 2—Lifeguard 5   Solo 3—Lifeguard 6
I'm Guilty
    Solo 1—boy   Solo 2—girl
    Solo 3—boy or girl   Solo 4—boy or girl
Living Water
    Solo—Sandy   Solo—Dew
    Solo—Shelly   Solo—Tanner

Microphone Needs

It would be good to have a cordless lavaliere microphone for each main character. Hand-held microphones can be used as a substitute. Place three solo microphones on stands stage left to accommodate the solos.

Scripture References

Splash Kingdom
    John 7:38
        "Whoever believes in me, as the Scripture has said, streams of living water will flow from within him."

Do You Know Him?
    John 3:3
        In reply Jesus declared, "I tell you the truth, no one can see the kingdom of God unless he is born again. "

Lifesaving 101
    John 10:9
        "I am the gate; whoever enters through me will be saved."
    Acts 16:31
        They replied, "Believe in the Lord Jesus, and you will be saved--you and your household."

A. Admit you have sinned.

I'm Guilty

Romans 3:23

"For all have sinned and fall short of the glory of God."

B. Believe God Loves you and sent His Son Jesus to save you from your sins.

We Believe in Jesus Christ

John 3:16

"For God so loved the world that he gave his one and only Son, that whoever believes in him shall not perish but have eternal life."

C. Claim Jesus as Your Savior. Acknowledge God's forgiveness, respond with love, and follow Jesus.

Living Water

Romans 10:13

"Everyone who calls on the name of the Lord will be saved."

Bubbling Joy

Proverbs 18:4

"The words of a man's mouth are deep waters, but the fountain of wisdom is a bubbling brook."

Dive

Revelation 22:1-2

"Then the angel showed me the river of the water of life, as clear as crystal, flowing from the throne of God and of the Lamb down the middle of the great street of the city."

Finale (Come on in, the Water's Fine!/Splash Kingdom/We Believe in Jesus Christ/Dive)

Matthew 28:19-20

"Therefore go and make disciples of all nations, baptizing them in the name of the Father and of the Son and of the Holy Spirit, and teaching them to obey everything I have commanded you. And surely I am with you always, to the very end of the age."

THE CHILDREN OF YOUR COMMUNITY FOR CHRIST

WITH

THE STORY OF JESUS FOR CHILDREN

Lillenas Publishing Company and Campus Crusade for Christ have partnered together to help provide for you a tool to reach the children of your community. In conjunction with your presentation Splash Kingdom, why not plan an outreach event called

"Celebrate! Jesus for Children Day."

Campus Crusade has developed this program around the special children's 62-minute edition of the **Jesus Film** just for the purpose of reaching children and their families. With children telling the story, your children will witness the life and ministry of Jesus as found in the Gospel of Luke.

In the Splash Kingdom Resource Kit, we have provided a full CD–ROM that provides all of the resources necessary to host this program. Complete with training and promotional materials, this FREE CD-ROM will put you in touch with Campus Crusade for Christ and help you get your copy of The Story of Jesus for Children.

Only available in the
DIRECTOR'S RESOURCE KIT   MB-863 D
DIRECTOR'S RESOURCE KIT/VIDEO   MD-527